The Process

How to Experience a Life of Transformative Faith

Pastor Derrick L. McRae

Sermon To Book
www.sermontobook.com

The Process / Derrick L. McRae
ISBN-13: 978-1-945793-86-8

To all of those who have deposited into me.

CONTENTS

Foreword by Archbishop Allen T.D. Wiggins 3
For Our Good 7
Riding Out the Storm 15
Living Outside the Comfort Zone 33
Life Outside the Boat 55
Seek His Face 73
Acknowledgments 82
About the Author 85
About Sermon To Book 88
Notes 89

Foreword by
Archbishop Allen T.D. Wiggins

Conviction is birthed out of one's knowledge of truth. Truth can be discovered in many ways, but topping the list is personal experience. Mentors often advise aspiring authors to first "write about what they know." This advice is offered knowing that great writings usually come from the depth of an author's intimate personal experience with the subject they write about, which instantly establishes a connection with the reader, who in turn senses truth and conviction.

I have known Pastor Derrick McRae for decades, and I can attest to his declared convictions, as well as his passion for expressing his truth. Pastor Derrick has given me the privilege and permission to speak into his life, and I'm honored to witness his unfolding and his desire to bless others through his personal experiences.

I love writings that are filled with spiritual truths that remain relevant and applicable to daily living. *The Process* is a composite of Derrick McRae's journey and his life lessons gathered along the way.

Transparency can be rather risky, as it allows others to view your situation through their own personal lens. If given the opportunity, more often than not, the arbitration of perspectives can yield the settlement of misunderstandings or, at minimum, the appreciation of context. By sharing his story, Pastor McRae transforms a homily into a hearing by posing thought-provoking questions to spark a discussion that is intended to voice the views of others, ultimately leading to a reconciling moment of truth. At the end of each chapter, purposefully placed, are tools to assist you in your personal growth.

When we, as the body of believers, embrace maturity as an essential, whether spiritual or natural, then and only then can we find ourselves truly experiencing peace beyond typical reasoning. Even with a sincere desire to contribute to humanity and fulfill our purpose, we must consider the vast array of tests and trials, frequently regarded as setbacks, that cause us to ask the question, "Why me?" As time passes, we mature, reaching our time of seasoning, which allows us to have greater regard for all of the experiences that have, in fact, flavored the seasoning. We learn to treasure the process that has shaped us and made us who and what we are.

This is the foundation for the deep-seated passion conveyed in McRae's offering, which will touch the very depths of your soul. Revelation 12:11 says, "And they overcame him by the blood of the Lamb and by the word of their testimony, and they did not love their lives to the death" (NKJV). Jesus made His contribution, and in this book God allows the writer to present his installment towards the ultimate fulfillment of your divine assignment.

I recommend this book be purchased, read, studied, and digested. It is our prayer that you ponder its contents and be encouraged and inspired to embrace your challenges. May you extract from them the tools necessary to blaze your path through the storms you will encounter in this life.

Archbishop Allen T.D. Wiggins
Presiding Prelate of the +I+B+C+, Inc.
The Hope Church, Senior Pastor
Orlando, Florida

INTRODUCTION

For Our Good

So let's not get tired of doing what is good. At just the right time we will reap a harvest of blessing if we don't give up.

—Galatians 6:9

We often assume that following a path of righteousness means our lives will be filled with good fortune. Perhaps we feel this is our due for the sacrifices that such a path entails. Why shouldn't we be rewarded, after all, when we are striving to do what God asks of us?

Our expectations boil down to a simple equation: walking with God equals ease and comfort, while choosing sin translates to misery and unhappiness. However, life is never that clear-cut. For one thing, sin is not always unpleasant, certainly not in the moment. This truth that sin is sometimes appealing and pleasurable is not something we think about very much, because we are taught from a very young age that sin is bad. How can it be otherwise when it serves no other purpose than to align us with the devil?

But whether we like to think about it or not, there's a reason that people choose the devil's path. Sometimes, people who aren't walking with Christ seem quite happy and appear to be flourishing. Conversely, those who choose to follow Christ have, more often than not, stepped onto the path of suffering:

> *But as for me, I almost lost my footing. My feet were slipping, and I was almost gone. For I envied the proud when I saw them prosper despite their wickedness. They seem to live such painless lives; their bodies are so healthy and strong. They don't have troubles like other people; they're not plagued with problems like everyone else.*
>
> ***—Psalm 73:2–5***

Sin *is* bad, but sinfulness doesn't equal misery. To ignore this fact serves only to make our lives harder, as we box sin into something that is always one thing and never another.

An honest person will probably admit that there's at least one point in their life when they sinned—and enjoyed it. Sin may lead to damnation, but it can be downright fun at times. You probably know what I'm talking about. I'm sure there have been times when you have given into temptation in its many forms. The crazy part is, those sinful periods in your life may have seemed less stressful than the righteous path you follow now.

There's something else at work here—another misconception that clouds our thinking. Too often we expect an immediate reward for living an upright and just life. We tend to forget that our reward for following God comes at the end. As a result, we can become frustrated and even resentful in the face of our daily struggles and hardships. These feelings can impair our judgment and perspective to the point that we forget one important truth: bad times always pass.

Our reward will come in the form of eternal life:

> *For our present troubles are small and won't last very long. Yet they produce for us a glory that vastly outweighs them and will last forever!*
>
> ***—2 Corinthians 4:17***

Meanwhile, those who have taken the easier path will likewise reap what they sow in the end:

> *Though the wicked sprout like weeds and evildoers flourish, they will be destroyed forever.*
>
> ***—Psalm 92:7***

Without the benefit of this calming perspective, we may even slip into despair. We may feel trapped by our circumstances, as though we are inching closer and closer to ruin. The devil is just waiting for these weak moments, these small windows of opportunity, to drive a wedge between God and us.

You may be in the midst of such a time of crisis. You've committed to Christ but still find yourself challenged by situations in your life. Especially during these moments, remember what Romans 8:28 tells us: God works in all things, even our difficulties, *for our own good.*

> *And we know that God causes everything to work together for the good of those who love God and are called according to his purpose for them.*
>
> ***—Romans 8:28***

That's right. God is aware of the struggles inherent in following His path—He may even be *choosing* to challenge us through them. As strange as it sounds, we can take solace in that knowledge. If we accept that God put these storms in our path for a reason, then we can find the strength and resolve to ride them out. We know He is with us through each storm and is still there for us when the skies clear.

In this book, we'll explore what it looks like to have the kind of faith that enables you to walk on water during a storm. At the end of each chapter, workbook sections will help you apply these principles to your life in a practical way.

I ask you to keep Romans 8:28 in mind as you read this book and even as you struggle with fear and frustration throughout your life. Take a deep breath and remind yourself that God won't leave you to face your challenges and hard times alone, any more than He did the men and women whom He has challenged before you.

WORKBOOK

Introduction Questions

Question: How does the perceived connection between righteousness and happiness sometimes differ from a person's reality?

Question: When and what is the reward for a righteous life?

____

____

____

____

____

____

____

____

____

____

____

____

Action: Memorize Romans 8:28 and meditate on it as you begin this study.

Introduction Notes

CHAPTER ONE

Riding Out the Storm

When Jesus woke up, he rebuked the wind and said to the waves, "Silence! Be still!" Suddenly the wind stopped, and there was a great calm. Then he asked them, "Why are you afraid? Do you still have no faith?"

—Mark 4:39–40

In Mark 4:35–41, the apostles found themselves literally led into a storm by following God. After a day of preaching before a large crowd, Jesus asked to be taken away to pray and reflect. He and His apostles set out by ship across the sea, but as Jesus slept below deck, a violent storm began to rage over the water. The sky darkened menacingly, the wind roared and huge waves crashed over the decks of the boat. Yet still Jesus slept.

The apostles were sure that death was near. As their small boat was tossed to and fro, they prepared for the worst—and then they remembered something. Confused, they said to themselves, "Wait a minute, this was Jesus' idea. He led us right into this storm, and now He's napping peacefully while we're up here almost drowning."

Or, to put their words in a context that may sound familiar, they asked, "God, we did what You wanted, so why are we in this mess?"

Finally, in their desperation and fear, the apostles went below deck to wake Jesus. What they said to Him is very telling: "Teacher, don't you care that we're going to drown?" (Mark 4:38).

Consider this for a moment. In the midst of a great storm threatening to sink their boat, with the wind whipping and the waves beating like hammers against the ship, the first thing the apostles said to Jesus wasn't, "Hey, Lord, how about a little help here so we don't drown?" but rather, "Master, don't You care about us?"

"Don't You love us? Or is it all a lie?"

We all know how this story ends. Jesus gets up from His nap and tells the sea to settle down and it does, because even the sea knows better than to disobey God. But what's interesting about this story, what resonates with us today, is the apostles' twofold reaction: *"Why is this happening?"* and *"Doesn't God care about us?"*

Why Us?

I have told you all this so that you may have peace in me. Here on earth you will have many trials and sorrows. But take heart, because I have overcome the world.

—John 16:33

In my tough times, in my painful trials, I have pondered these exact same questions, and I'm sure you have too. I can remember it like yesterday: I had stepped out in faith based on what I thought were God's directions concerning my future. I served God with all my heart and walked in obedience of His assignments for me. Then, on the cusp of the most faith-challenging moment I had ever experienced, I saw my entire life shift.

When I began my ministry, I heard many dreadful stories of how members of my generation had attempted to start their ministries and faced challenges from their pastors. However, I assumed these challenges were due to my peers' disrespectful methods and dishonest tactics. So, my desire was to be different. I wanted to be the example of leaving the right way and maintaining a great relationship with my previous pastor.

I set up a meeting and—with butterflies in my stomach, yet conviction in my heart—I walked into his office. I told my pastor exactly what I felt the Lord leading me to do. To the best of my ability, I explained the vision God had given me and the conviction I had to carry out my assignment.

The conversation went extremely well. My pastor praised my gifts and my service to his ministry, but more importantly, he looked me in the eyes and said, "If anyone in this church is qualified to pastor, it is you." Those words felt so good! I had previously served under another pastor who had seemingly dedicated his life to destroying my confidence in ministry, but now I was being validated. I had never experienced such validation before and the feeling was electric. I shed a tear as I saw the work of God unfolding right before my eyes.

Two days later, I received a phone call directly from my senior pastor inviting me to lunch. We went to our favorite place to eat at that time, a nice restaurant in Orlando called Johnson's Diner. I was feeling great—the Lord was moving.

But then suddenly my entire life shifted drastically. My pastor said to me, "I've thought a little more about what we talked about the other day, and I think it would be best if you just moved on with your ministry."

My jaw dropped as I sat there in disbelief. All I could think about was the fact that I had three kids, one in high school and two in private school, and a wife who worked in the education field.

This was my *"Why me?"* moment. After all of the hard work I had rendered, after all of the good seeds I had sown, all of the denial of rest I had given to the success of the ministry from which I was now being released, it was an extremely difficult moment for me.

To add insult to injury, I found myself falling behind in every bill I had. My wife and I hid our cars in the garage in order to keep them from being repossessed due to late payments. Our utilities were disconnected each month. It was a tough season, but God began to show me His ability to teach in the midst of a storm.

It is amazing how we can become so blinded by what we are experiencing that we don't realize the hand of God and the people that He often uses to push us into our destiny. My first thought was to be offended and frustrated due to my own self-righteous mentality. But once I had a moment to settle myself and ask the "why," I learned that this was the "how." Many of us desire the "what" but hate the "how." In hindsight, I truly believe with all of the good that my pastor did for me, with all of the wisdom that he shared with me and with all of the resources that he provided for my family and me, this was a great act of God through my pastor. It took years to understand the wisdom of my pastor to push me into my promise.

Many people believe we learn from God in the good seasons of life, but I've found that some of my most intimate moments with God have come in the most trying seasons of life. It was in my lowest moment that 2 Corinthians 12:9 became a reality: "Each time he said, 'My grace is all you need. My power works best in weakness.' So now

I am glad to boast about my weaknesses, so that the power of Christ can work through me."

I personally found the hand of God to be enough to carry me over the finish line. God was simply showing me, "I have you covered." That season of lack and struggle has proven to be necessary for where I've arrived in ministry. I'm sure it is true in your life as well that there have been moments or seasons when it felt like the wind and the waves threatened to completely capsize you, and in those times you cried out, "Why is this happening? Doesn't God care about me?"

There are no easy answers to these questions—usually the answers we're given feel cheap or insincere. "God is testing you," or "It's important to find joy even in these difficult times," are the types of responses that can be difficult to navigate.

But there are better, deeper and truer answers for our questions when the storms of life hit.

Let us start with the first question: *Why is this happening?*

Like the apostles trapped on that stormy sea in the Gospel of Mark, we choose to follow God the best that we can. We have stepped willingly onto the ship and set the course He charted for us. Yet still bad things happen—sometimes *very* bad things. During these moments, we may wonder if we should have gotten on the boat with God in the first place!

At these times, however, we need to ask

ourselves a couple of hard questions before we shake our fists at God or accuse Him of abandoning us.

- Why did we think things would be so easy in the first place?
- Did God actually promise us a safe, calm passage through life, or did we create this expectation on our own?

Of course, when we ask tough questions, we get tough answers, and the answer that you are likely to run into is that God didn't bring these difficulties into your life. Sometimes we bring difficulties upon ourselves, and sometimes going through trials is just part of being human.

Note that once Jesus was awakened, He gave no indication that the storm was unexpected or a problem. He wasn't surprised or rushed. He rose, calmed the storm, and then, in what seems to be frustration, asked His disciples why they had been so afraid. After all, His original direction was that they were going to "the other side" of the lake. His hope was that they would have believed Him and continued through the storm, knowing that if Jesus had said they were going to the other side, then they would be going to the other side, regardless of the wind and the waves and the danger.

Did you get that? Jesus said they were going to the other side, but He didn't say it would be easy or pleasant.

Nowhere in the Bible does God promise that being saved means we will be spared any difficulties. In 2 Corinthians 12:7b, Paul says, "to keep me from becoming proud, I was given a thorn in my flesh, a messenger from Satan to torment me and keep me from becoming proud." Paul acknowledged that this thorn was given to him to help him remain humbled. Remember, this is after his conversion, which shows us that having become new in Christ does not mean you won't be enticed to entertain what was a familiar behavior in your old life. Your suffering is not necessarily an indication of something wrong you've done. The truth is, all will suffer.

Job 14:1 says, "How frail is humanity! How short is life, how full of trouble!" There is no place on earth safe from strife. In fact, you can have problems on your way to church! Perhaps you receive terrible news about a family member or a big opportunity you hoped would come through. Perhaps you lose a job or you lose a friend. You may lose your Christian joy because the house is messy, the kids are acting up, or you didn't get the days off you had hoped for.

Being saved is not an insurance policy against any and all kinds of trouble. In fact, this misconception can make our lives even harder because, in our disillusionment, we fail to see that life is a cycle of good times and bad. We start to focus only on the negatives, until it seems as though there is nothing *but* stress and tribulation. This inevitably leads us to consider the very question the apostles asked Jesus when they woke Him from sleep.

Does God Even Care?

It is important to remember that the men on that boat with Jesus were closer to Him than anybody. They'd spent time with Him every day, heard Him preach, witnessed countless miracles, and yet they reacted exactly the way we do in the midst of our struggles. They asked, in panic and desperation, "Master, carest thou not that we perish?" (Mark 4:38 KJV).

It's important to note the term *master.* They used this term because they had seen Jesus heal the blind, the lame, and the sick. They had witnessed His incredible love for others, and because of that love, they called Him *master,* often translated as "teacher" (for example, Mark 4:38 NLT). It was a term of extreme respect for the One who had shown such compassion and love.

And yet here they were in the boat, questioning that very love, because a storm threatened their lives.

To be clear, the apostles were not really asking, "Don't You care about us?" The evidence that God cares about His followers is as abundant in their lives as it is in ours. The fact that you woke up this morning at all, much less with a roof over your head and food to eat and clothes to wear, is evidence enough of God's concern. Of course, Jesus cared about His apostles, just like God cares about us.

The real question the apostles were asking is the same one that we ask in our times of difficulty: "Don't You care about *me*?" Much like His followers in the Gospels, we want the assurance that God is paying attention to our individual problems and struggles and needs at all times. We crave the assurance that He is going to fix our lives for us so that we can relax, breathe easy, and enjoy nonstop good times.

At our worst, we may even turn to our neighbors and make assumptions about their lives from our outside vantage point. It's easy enough to do. We peek through our windows at their big houses, make snap judgments about the nice clothes they wear and the fancy cars they drive. In truth, this doesn't tell us anything of substance about their lives or the crosses they bear in secret. But it's a useful tool if we want to confirm our own suspicions that that they somehow have it easier than we do.

In this way, we convince ourselves that our neighbors' lives are better, that God has set them up to succeed. If this is the case, and we've already told ourselves that it is, then we assume that our deliverance must be coming next. And when that doesn't happen—or when it doesn't happen according to our preferred timeline—our misplaced sense of envy grows into something worse.

The truth is that God sets all of us up to succeed, even if we do not recognize it in the moment. What we fail to realize or, in some cases, struggle to accept, is that even our trials are designed to help us.

He Hasn't Abandoned You

God does not raise us up to suffer. He raises us up to conquer our suffering. Just because He does not prevent every moment of strife and every single obstacle does not mean that God has forgotten about you. He knows exactly where you are and what you are enduring, just as Jesus knew even in His sleep what the apostles were facing during that storm.

Yet still we wait, just like the apostles waited for Him, to fix our problems or to remove us from our difficult situations. We sit and stew in our sadness and fear, waiting wordlessly for Him to deliver us. Perhaps we even grow resentful when He does not answer the prayers we haven't offered!

Mark's story of the storm is the perfect illustration of this behavior. The dark clouds gathered and the apostles waited. The wind howled louder, the water continued to rise, but only when the boat was about to sink did the apostles go below the deck to wake Jesus. They went to Him as a last resort, when they should have trusted Him all along. They should have held on to the fact that Jesus had called them to go to the other side of the lake. He was in charge of the trip from the start. Trust should have been their first and only response.

In the end, God delivered the apostles from harm, just as He delivers us. However, His methods are not always as simple or direct as a word or two to calm the storm. Sometimes we miss His quiet guidance in the midst of life's chaos. Sometimes we miss the miracle God uses to deliver us from danger. And sometimes that miracle is ourselves.

God empowers us to face the sudden storms. He wants us to use our faith to stare them down, not unlike Jesus did on that ship. The power to do this lies within each of us, because God put it there. Our greatest challenge is to remember this, even when we are not at our best. And we're rarely at our best in times of crisis. We panic and ponder while our tempers are often as short as our memories.

We need these memories above all to remind ourselves that we've been here before. With God's help and guidance, we have faced other dark times and survived them. These past experiences are an important tool, not just for us, but also for each other.

Every time God leads us back to the safe harbor or empowers us to find it ourselves, we become a comforting example to our brothers and sisters who may be dealing with similar circumstances. In this way, we become living, breathing testimonials that dark times will pass and that God remains by our side even when it seems like He is sleeping below the decks. And in reminding our neighbors of this, we also remind ourselves for the next time the cycle repeats and it is once again our turn to face hardships.

WORKBOOK

Chapter One Questions

Question: In the midst of a dangerous storm, what was the question most bothering the disciples? Describe a time when you questioned God's personal care for you.

Question: What are some common answers people give in times of trial and difficulty? Where do those responses fall short?

____

____

____

____

____

____

____

____

____

____

____

____

Question: Why do Christians sometimes have an expectation that their lives will not have trouble? When have you been surprised by suffering? When have you compared your life to another's (thinking they had an easier, better life) without knowing all the facts?

____

____

____

____

____

____

____

____

____

____

____

____

Question: What was the attitude that Jesus wanted the disciples to have in the storm? What are some of God's purposes for His people in going through life's storms?

____

____

____

____

____

____

____

____

____

____

____

Action: Create a "Thankful Journal" that documents all of the things, big and small, that reveal God's goodness in your life. This can include anything from having money to buy groceries for the week to seeing a sunset that comforts you. In this journal, you can also write Bible verses that bring you peace as you think of them or as you encounter them while reading God's Word.

You can also use this journal to document testimonies of storms that God sees you through.

When you experience challenging circumstances, you can read through your "Thankful Journal" and be reminded of God's faithfulness.

Chapter One Notes

CHAPTER TWO

Living Outside the Comfort Zone

> *As Pharaoh approached, the people of Israel looked up and panicked when they saw the Egyptians overtaking them. They cried out to the LORD, and they said to Moses, "Why did you bring us out here to die in the wilderness? Weren't there enough graves for us in Egypt? What have you done to us? Why did you make us leave Egypt?*
>
> ***—Exodus 14:10–11***

Sometimes following God can put us in the midst of trouble, as the apostles found out in Mark's story of the storm. In other cases, we may think God is leading us into trouble when, in truth, He's actually trying to save us, if we're just willing to listen to Him.

Such is the situation with the Israelites early in the Old Testament. In Exodus 14:10–31, the Israelites were beginning to unravel. They had been on the run from Pharaoh's army for what seemed like an eternity. Every day, they felt him getting closer. They could almost hear his chariots, feel his spears, taste the sand that would surely fill their mouths when they fell.

All around them was desert. They were starving, exhausted. And yet they could not sleep. They could not think. They only knew the paralyzing fear that gripped them.

They ran until they were out of room to run any further. On one side, the unforgiving Red Sea—more or less, two hundred miles across at its widest point and well over a mile deep at its deepest point. There was no such thing as swimming across this sea. And there certainly was no easy way to cross tens of thousands of people by boat in a short amount of time.

On the other side, Pharaoh. His rage had been building. He wanted Moses and the Israelites to pay.

The Israelites felt trapped. This was their breaking point.

There are times in our lives when we feel much the same way, even if our circumstances are typically far less dramatic. Sure, we've all been caught between a "rock and a hard place" at one time or another, but few of us have ever been stuck between a bloodthirsty army and the sea.

Still, in our fear and frustration, we might find ourselves responding like the Israelites who questioned Moses: "Why did we follow you into this mess?" Though really, they were talking directly to God, essentially saying: "Weren't we better off as slaves in Egypt? At least in those days, Pharaoh wasn't trying to kill us!" (Exodus 14:10–12).

Their reaction may seem understandable, until you consider what their lives actually were like *before*. In Egypt the Israelites were slaves, and Pharaoh was their cruel master. They were worked mercilessly, whipped and beaten—sometimes for no reason at all. They were only slightly less hungry and certainly just as miserable than before God intervened. He saw their torment and freed them by sending plague after plague down upon the Egyptians until Pharaoh had no choice but to let the Israelites go (Exodus 7–12).

Not only that, but He also led them out of Egypt with an abundance.

> *And the people of Israel did as Moses had instructed; they asked the Egyptians for clothing and articles of silver and gold. The LORD caused the Egyptians to look favorably on the Israelites, and they gave the Israelites whatever they asked for. So they stripped the Egyptians of their wealth!*
>
> ***—Exodus 12:35–36***

All of this was quickly forgotten, however, when the children of Israel looked out and saw Pharaoh's men bearing down on one side and the impassable Red Sea looming on the other. They failed to remember how bad their situation had been before all of this—and some of them even longed to return to slavery!

"Sure, our lives were miserable before," they thought, "but at least things were stable in Egypt. We were secure in slavery. We knew what would happen when we woke up in the morning and what awaited us the next day when we went to bed at night."

With these doubts weighing heavily on their minds, the Israelites started to question everything: their decision to escape, Moses' leadership, and even God's plan. Some of them undoubtedly wondered whether or not God even had *had* a plan when He set this rescue mission in motion!

This kind of thinking may sound crazy to us from a distance; certainly the idea of choosing slavery over freedom does. But in reality, our minds work much the same way when we contemplate our own struggles. Far too many of us choose to stay in unhealthy or even dangerous situations rather than free ourselves, even as God urges us to do just that.

Justifying Unhappiness

Life, as we have already discussed, is a cycle of good times and bad. No one is immune to the latter, those valleys between the peaks, not even those of us who dedicate ourselves to God.

You have experienced this—weeks or months or maybe even whole years when it feels as though you are under attack. It could be attacks on your body in the form of physical ailments or illnesses, attacks on your finances or livelihood, or even attacks against your way of life. Sometimes there are sneak attacks, such as when you are betrayed by a loved one, or attacks of loneliness caused by lack of affection and human contact. Perhaps you feel attacked simply by the fear of not having the information or support you need to deal with a particular problem.

We all face these things, and we try to battle them as best we can, even when we seem destined to lose. Sometimes we do lose a particular battle; sometimes the attack is simply too much for us to withstand. There may be nothing we can do to avoid these situations, but as Christians we need to keep our wits about us. We must remember that these attacks pass, and even at their worst, even with the ones we may have lost, God always has our backs.

Part of that understanding, that faith we have in God, is being able to recognize when He is trying to help us by leading us away from these situations. He did this for Israel. In the midst of their problems, when it seemed impossible, God made a path by splitting open the Red Sea. At the same time, He held the enemy at bay with a great cloud. He made a path while also having their backs, so to speak.

Though the Israelites couldn't help but see the path God created through the Red Sea, we do not always catch the road signs He's putting down to aid our way out of crisis or trouble. And sometimes, even when we do see them, we hesitate to follow them out of fear.

The truth is, we like comfort, and there can be comfort even in our misery. Some of us wake up every day and curse our jobs. We hate going to work, but ten years later, fifteen years later, there we still are, trudging into the office every morning with frowns on our faces.

Like the Israelites toiling away in Egypt, we may recognize that our lives are unhappy, but we may still be reluctant to change them. Familiar unhappiness can seem preferable to the terrifying unknown. Sometimes the devil himself whispers in our ears in an effort to keep our feet planted firmly in the mud; he wants desperately to scare us into staying put, because we're more vulnerable in these moments.

Going back to our example from the Bible, Pharaoh was just like Satan. Satan holds us in bondage and promises us just barely enough to survive. He says that we can leave our life of sin any time we want, but when we do, he chases us down and tries to drag us back into his lifestyle of sin. He is a powerful captor, and we find ourselves resisting God's command to escape rather than obey. We find ways to tell ourselves that our lives are not as bad as we think they are. "God, are You crazy?" we ask. "You're telling me to go when what's out there may be *worse* than what I've got going on now!" After all, we know where we are now. We've survived this long in our current situation, however unpleasant it may be. Why would we leave and risk making our lives even worse?

This attitude—this fear—means that we are forgetting what God has done for us before and what He'll do again if only we have faith. It means that God has to help us reshape our thinking before He can even help us escape our current challenges and difficulties.

When God Says Go, You GO!

In Exodus 14:13, God reminded the Israelites through Moses that He was on their side.

God spoke through Moses saying, "Don't be afraid. Just stand still and watch the LORD rescue you today. The Egyptians you see today will never be seen again" (Exodus 14:13). In other words, God promises to save the Israelites from Pharaoh's army, the same men who once enslaved them.

He commanded Moses to lift his rod and stretch out his hand, which Moses did, and just like that, the Red Sea parted (Exodus 14:15, 21–22). The waters separated to allow the Israelites a path to escape. And when the Egyptians attempted to follow, God sent the waters crashing back down upon them and their horses. The Egyptians drowned and the Israelites escaped for good.

We can learn a great deal from the story of this miracle. The first and most obvious lesson is that God backs up His promises.

Someone who actually follows through on what they say they're going to do is a rarity. We are so used to being let down, being lied to, and being forgotten that we've almost come to anticipate those very actions from God.

But God never breaks a promise. What He says He will do, He does (Numbers 23:19). In Exodus 14:14a, just before the Red Sea parted, Moses promised the Israelites, "The LORD himself will fight for you." Moses was assuring his frightened people that God didn't send all those plagues down on Pharaoh and the Egyptians, and He didn't deliver them from slavery and keep them alive in the desert just to abandon them when things got dire.

Though we don't face situations quite like the Israelites did in Exodus, there are times when it certainly feels like we are in a desert of some sort. There are times when our struggles seem physically impossible to endure. We wonder how we will ever get through the death of a loved one, the loss of a job, the betrayal of a friend. And yet here we still are, and there's only one reason: God delivers us.

I can remember losing my father during my final year of college. He was the primary breadwinner of our household. He was also extremely creative, a go-getter, my twin, and a wonderful guy to run ideas by. I had two younger siblings, my brother Darius, who is eighteen years younger than I am, and my baby sister Elise, who is twenty-three years younger than I am. My mom really hadn't worked much, as my father had extended to her the opportunity to assist him with his company.

To say the least, it was a frightening time during which I did not know what the future had to present for our family. However, I remember saying to myself one day as I was driving down the street, "If God had planned for me to be a failure, it would have happened by now." I then began to think back to previous victories and the doors the Lord had opened for me in the past.

Before I knew it, a sense of peace came over me. I knew within my heart that everything would work out according to God's plan. It was that day, that moment, that I made a promise to myself to always find something positive in the midst of whatever I face. Philippians 4:8 tells us, "Fix your thoughts on what is true, and honorable, and right, and pure, and lovely, and admirable. Think about things that are excellent and worthy of praise." Often, we don't lose due to our obstacles as much as we lose due to how we view the obstacles we face.

The aforementioned trial gave space for God's ability to manifest within my life. Be encouraged:

whenever major shifts occur in your life, look for the positioning of God in the process. It has proven to be true for me that life will deliver sudden, unexpected changes to our comfortable systems and patterns, but God has a plan for our outcome. God's plan makes us "better" not "bitter."

These are precisely the moments we need to remember when we feel hesitant to leave our present difficulties. By remembering, we find the courage to see where God is trying to lead us. This can be harder than it seems because our vision gets cloudy at times. It becomes obscured by our fears and insecurities and stress. Fear weakens our ability to see, creating a special kind of tunnel vision that's almost like being in an incapacitated state. In these moments, we may fixate on the problem in front of us—that big dark cloud blocking out the light the way the moon blocks the sun during an eclipse.

That cloud isn't the only problem. The truth is, even when our vision is 20/20, we still never see as clearly as God does. He sees the whole picture in a way we never will. The Bible tells us this. In Jeremiah 29:11, the Lord says, "For I know the plans I have for you … plans to prosper you and not to harm you, plans to give you hope and a future" (NIV). In other words, *God knows what He's doing*. He knows exactly when and how to move us from one place to the next, which makes our jobs that much easier. All we need to do is listen and follow.

God Knows Where We Need to Be, Even If We Don't

Accepting God's plan is the first step in our journey, not the end of it. That journey will not always be comfortable. The Israelites who followed Moses out of Egypt learned this lesson the hard way. They spent day after day and year after year wandering through the desert, surviving on quail and manna while they slowly lost their faith in God's plan.

This fact bears repeating: God did *not* lead the Israelites directly from slavery to prosperity, nor will He bring us instantly from a bad situation into a great one. We would prefer that, of course. We would love to be able to approve God's plan for us ahead of time, as though it were a vacation itinerary. That way we can know exactly what to expect, maybe even cross off some of the activities we don't feel like doing. But God's plan is not our plan, and He's not looking for our input.

As such, we must endure a period of uncertainty and transition as we put our faith in Him. That period may be downright uncomfortable—but it's *supposed* to be uncomfortable. God is leading us from one realm of faith to another. He's testing us, stretching our faith.

It may sound crazy, but this experience is good

for us. Growth occurs during new experiences, not familiar ones. Our faith stagnates when everything is the same, when we can predict, good or bad, what will happen the next day and the day after that. This stagnation only makes it harder to accept the lessons God is trying to impart to us.

We need change to grow, because change tests our limits. It challenges us, and through that process, our faith in God grows. *We* grow and become more self-sufficient. Sometimes God helps us in ways that may feel just as miraculous as the parting of the Red Sea, while, in other cases, it can be a lot less obvious. Many times, He helps us simply by revealing the strength within ourselves that we didn't know existed. But God knew it was there because He put it in us.

Trust in Him

In Exodus, the Israelites put their faith in God (through Moses) to lead them out of Egypt. Like them, we must put our faith in His plan for us, no matter how risky that plan may seem. If God tells us it's time to leave our present situation, then we need to pack our bags and hit the road. The journey He has planned for us will test our strength and resolve, just as it tested the Israelites. It may leave us hungry and thirsty and desperate.

Most importantly, it may lead us to a dead end—or a moment that feels like a dead end. The Israelites faced this at the Red Sea, with

Pharaoh's men and scary horse-drawn chariots ready to drag them back to Egypt or even trample them in the sand.

Our period of transition *always* comes with a crucial test. This is the point where we become convinced we made a mistake, or worse, that God may have. We then have two options. The first is the one the Israelites chose initially. We can moan and complain, or even question our decision to follow God by leaving a bad situation for one that seems even worse.

Or we can hearken back once more to Romans 8:28: "And we know that in all things God works for the good of those who love him, who have been called according to his purpose" (NIV). It's such a simple message that we may be tempted to dismiss as trivial. However, the simplest messages are often the truest: everything that happens, good and bad, *is* God working on our behalf. We just can't always see how He is working in the stress of that moment.

When the Lord told me to start The Experience Christian Center, He called me from a very comfortable place under a trailblazer of a leader. I had experienced tremendous growth and seen God's hand working in my ministry. In all honesty, I had become comfortable and accustomed to greatness.

Growing up in the Church of God in Christ and now leading a great work within the Missionary Baptist Church had given me a solid base with a tremendous network. I was okay with becoming a pastor, but my desire was to inherit or take over a ministry that was already functioning, not to start one from scratch. My request of God was simple: that He give me the two Bs, a building and a budget. I had already played this scenario in my mind.

But God had a different plan. In September 2009, I called a group of individuals together to talk about what God had called me to do. This team consisted of individuals I had known for years and some who were basically fed up with the church world as they knew it. None of these individuals had ever held a position within a church, but all believed in the vision God had given to me.

So in December of 2009, on the last day of the year, we launched our ministry. It was an amazing night—over 700 people attended. It looked like God's plan was going to be carried out with ease. I can remember telling a few of the team leaders, "we've done great tonight, but this is not what it looks like." After the dust had settled, we finally started our ministry with just twenty-two individuals, excluding my three kids.

We had nothing but a vision to produce a great work for God. It was a terrifying situation, as I fully recognized that starting this ministry would take me away from my full-time position as a youth pastor, which, for many of my colleagues, was a dream situation. I led one of the most recognized youth ministries in my city. We had a very liberal budget that helped make youth ministry happen, and I had the perfect staff surrounding the vision God had given me.

However, my fear of walking in disobedience was stronger than any worry I could have had about leaving a perfect situation behind. So I stepped out and started my new ministry with no source of income or backing for the development of the ministry.

For three years, I witnessed God provide for me without me ever asking one member for assistance. It was God's way of proving to me what "Faith in Action" could produce. This transition gave me confidence in the ability of God that prepared me for what was to come in ministry. I actually grew not only financially, but there also was great growth and development spiritually. This process was exactly what I needed to prepare me for who and what was to come in ministry.

James 1:4 says, "So let it grow, for when your endurance is fully developed, you will be perfect and complete, needing nothing." That text spoke to me so often when I considered what God had said and where I was. However, I had to grasp that God was preparing me to be able to fulfill what He had set in motion.

This remains our challenge during our crucial test. When things are at their worst, we have to acknowledge our need for God instead of giving up on Him. After all, He never gives up on us.

He's always watching, always protecting us, even as He challenges us to grow our faith. And it's at these most trying of times, the times when we feel the most desperate and alone, that God comes through with the miracle.

A miracle can't happen without a mess. No one needs a miracle when life is perfect. If your marriage is going well and your kids are happy and acing all their tests at school and your boss gives you a raise every six months, you don't have much need for a miracle.

It is only at those moments of greatest stress, that same breaking point the Israelites reached in the desert, when God reveals Himself. He asks us to heed His plan, to take a leap of faith if we want to escape our difficulties. That leap is a continuation of the faith we placed in Him to begin our journey, and it is part of the ongoing trial He uses to strengthen that faith. And when we find ourselves out of resources and unable to continue, He is there to lift us up.

God continues to remind us, just as He reminded the Israelites, that we will not be overtaken. He will always find a path for us through our difficulties, even if it takes parting the very seas.

WORKBOOK

Chapter Two Questions

Question: Far too many of us choose to stay in unhealthy or even dangerous situations rather than free ourselves, even as God urges us to do just that. Describe a time when you chose "familiar unhappiness" over the "terrifying unknown." What has to happen inside a person before he or she is willing to make a life change?

____

____

____

____

____

____

____

____

____

____

____

____

Question: Describe the difference between God's perspective on your life and present difficulties versus your perspective? What are some reasons you can trust God?

____

____

____

____

____

____

____

____

____

____

____

____

Question: What is the purpose of the uncomfortable process between leaving your bondage and entering your promised land? How does the pain of change ultimately help you?

Question: Describe a time when you stepped forward in faith only to reach what seemed like a dead end. How did God prove Himself to you during this crucial test?

____

____

____

____

____

Action: What are areas where you need to change? Are there unhealthy personal habits such as diet and exercise, financial choices regarding debt and savings, or relationships in your life that need to go? Choose one of these areas and ask God to change your thinking so that you reject your self-imposed bondage and take the uncomfortable but necessary steps to freedom.

____

____

____

____

____

____

____

____

____

____

____

Chapter Two Notes

CHAPTER THREE

Life Outside the Boat

We're living in a time when people make assumptions about things as they appear to be. We look at people who are attractive and we assume they will make great husbands or wives. We look at people with wealth and success, and we assume that those people are happy. We look at certain jobs, and we assume that they bring satisfaction. We look at people who receive great opportunities, and we assume that those opportunities just fell into their laps.

Appearances shape the imagination of the mind. They paint a picture of a situation, despite little to no actual facts. There have been moments when I've scrolled down my timelines and viewed many of my social media friends' news feeds, and I was amazed with the external presentation of the success of many of their lives.

I've come to understand that people very rarely

post the reality of their lives. Many use social media platforms as a confidence builder, while others may use it to validate themselves. Some may engage to measure their level of success, but very few use it to communicate the total story of their true quality of life. We must be extremely careful not to draw conclusions of situations based on the status someone posts about. If we aren't careful, their appearance can subconsciously create unjust thoughts concerning the treatment of God toward our life in comparison to the favor displayed in their lives.

Growing up, my favorite television show was *The Cosby Show*, one of the most watched television shows of the mid-'80s to early '90s. The show centered around the lives of the Huxtables. The father, Dr. Cliff Huxtable, and mother, Claire Huxtable, had five children. They had the perfect house, the ideal relationship, perfect communication, wonderful parenting skills, a great neighborhood, all the money they needed, and educated children. It was the perfect family story.

As I grew older, I can remember desiring this seemingly perfect set up. I would say things like, "When I get married, I want to live and be just like this model television family." Well, over twenty years later, I've learned an important lesson: what happened on the show was suited for entertainment, and that image lasted only thirty minutes, including commercial breaks. I, too, could manage a perfect relationship with my wife for twenty-one minutes. The moral of the story is that the appearance can look better than the reality.

The word *appearance* is defined as "the way someone or something looks."[1] It's also the preconceived perception of the outcome of a particular situation. In other words, it's arriving at conclusions before the journey has been made or the circumstance has played out.

Our tendency to make assumptions based on appearance is only getting worse. We're living in a time of prejudice, a time of prejudgment. A time when so often we shut out the facts and block out possible explanations because we would rather perceive the problem through our own very limited lens.

Why Did You Doubt?

> *But Jesus spoke to them at once. "Don't be afraid," he said. "Take courage. I am here!"*
>
> ***—Matthew 14:27***

In Matthew 14, this problem of drawing a conclusion based on perception is exactly what happened to the disciples. They just witnessed an incredible miracle. Jesus, their leader, had taken five loaves of bread and two fish and used those items to feed a multitude of five thousand people.

The disciples saw the whole thing unfold

before them. In moments, the crowd had gone from asking for food to being pleasantly full, and it was all because of the man Jesus.

But Jesus was weary. He had been preaching and teaching, and He needed a break. So, when He instructed the disciples to take some time out on the Sea of Galilee while He prayed in the mountains, they obliged. After all, they too, needed some time of prayer and reflection after what they had just seen.

The disciples went into the boat into the middle of the lake. The wind was stronger there, and the water was more aggressive. But then, out on the horizon, they saw a man coming toward them. He was literally walking on the water.

"It's a ghost!" they cried out (Matthew 14:26).

But Jesus responded, "It is I" (Matthew 14:27 NIV).

The disciples gasped. Could it really be Him? Could Jesus really be walking on the water? I've learned in my early span of ministry that God will expose you to great things to prepare you for great trials. Always remember, with God nothing just happens. Psalm 37:23a teaches us that "The LORD directs the steps of the godly." Whenever you experience amazing or discomforting situations, know that what you face is never the full extent. God is always preparing you for something bigger than what you see.

Peter dared to call out, "Lord, if it's really you, tell me to come to you, walking on the water"

(Matthew 14:28).

The disciples were silent. Why did Peter just ask such a thing? Didn't he know the dangers of getting out of the boat in the middle of the lake during a storm? Often, those with strong opinions are really dressing up their regret for your confidence. You must learn to move beyond their fear and live out your personal conviction.

Jesus told Peter to come (Matthew 14:29).

The disciples couldn't believe what they were witnessing. They watched Peter as he swung one leg over the side of the boat, then the other. And then … he was standing. He was standing on the water. He took one step forward. Then he took another.

Peter was walking on the water, too. He was walking toward Jesus.

The wind picked up. The waves threatened, and Peter's gaze shifted to the trouble around him. He fell into the water, barely able to keep his head above the surface. "Save me, Lord!" he cried out (Matthew 14:30).

Jesus caught him before the words fully came out of his mouth.

"Why did you doubt me?" (Matthew 14:31). Jesus looked at Peter and then shifted His gaze to the other disciples. "Why did you doubt me?" Those in the boat spoke negatively toward Peter, but when I look at him, I see one who decided, "If life is going to end for me today, I might as well take advantage of this moment." I also see someone who decided to try something different. Peter had come to this conclusion as he maxed out his potential on the ship. He knew more existed and he decided to do something strange to obtain it.

Often, we dismiss ourselves from supernatural encounters with God because we refuse to stretch out and experience new levels with Him. If Peter had never exercised his faith, we today would not have the privilege of growing through this faith encounter.

God Works for Us

Sometimes I wonder what the conversation was like when Jesus separated Himself from the disciples. I wonder how the disciples took that. They saw Jesus perform a miracle, and suddenly He wanted some alone time. Did they take it personally? Did they think that Jesus was tired of them and their basic humanness?

Have you ever wondered what the thoughts of the Lord are concerning you? The enemy works overtime to twist the truth of God, to make us believe that God is working against us, and that there's no plan in place for Him to work for us.

If the truth be told, many of us question the motives of God. Many of us eventually come to a point where we believe that God really is working against us and that He doesn't like us. And so, instead of the church having a place of power and potential in this world, we find that the church becomes a place of pity and pain.

However, Jeremiah 29:11 tells us something different: "For I know the thoughts that I think toward you, saith the LORD, thoughts of peace, and not of evil, to give you an expected end" (KJV).

In the midst of this verse are two key phrases. The first key phrase—"the thoughts that I think toward you"—indicates that God wants to do something for you. He wants to work through you, and He wants to show Himself through you.

The second phrase, "to give you an expected end," includes the term *tiqvah*—literally, a cord, or figuratively, "thing that I long for"[2]—and *'achariyth*, which means "the last or end," "the future," or "posterity."[3] In understanding this promise, we must rest in knowing that God is always working for us and with us. Even when we find discomfort in His process, we must remember Romans 8:28: "And we know that in all things God works for the good of those who love him, who have been called according to his purpose."

He wants to fulfill His promises to you.

Sometimes you've just got to tell your mind that God isn't working against you. Rather, God is working for you. Sometimes you have to remind yourself that although you may be in a rough place right now, there's a purpose behind your placement.

Although you may be in a difficult time right now, it doesn't mean that this place you're in is your *final* place. It just means that you're resting for a bit. You're pausing here. It's a pitstop, not a parking garage. This is temporary.

When you really have a relationship with God, you understand this. You don't get nervous when things aren't working out the way you thought they were going to work out. When you really have a relationship with God, you understand that God intends to bring you out of what you're in and to bring you out with victory. You believe His promises and you trust His process.

Trust That Better Times Are Coming

I personally live life feeling like God's about to do something amazing for me. I feel like God wants to work something out. I feel potential. I feel like I'm going to the next level. I feel release. I feel that yokes are being broken. I feel chains falling. I feel God working.

You can live like this, too. Through God's grace, you can experience this second opportunity. Yesterday may have been a complete mess, but today is a new day. You have a new mind. You have a new passion, a new purpose. You have a new vision. You're open to new revelation, and you're casting off anything that tries to remind you of the past. You recognize that the worst is over, that Jesus keeps His promises, and that the best is yet to come, even though you still may have to go through some really tough stuff to get there. The best is yet to come. Praise God.

Purpose Versus Placement

Your word is a lamp to guide my feet and a light for my path.

—Psalm 119:105

The disciples had a hard time remembering that the best is still to come. They were listening to Jesus, and they were in the boat on the lake, but when Jesus revealed even more of Himself to them, they were stuck. Only one of them dared to get out of the boat. Only one of them trusted what was before him so wholeheartedly that he was willing to put it all on the line, believing that Jesus wouldn't let him down.

Peter didn't know how he was going to walk on water. He didn't understand the miraculous physics at work. He didn't need to.

There are times when you won't be able to see where you are going either. You won't understand how things can possibly work out in your favor, and yet you dare to take that step anyway. You dare to trust that your purpose is greater than your placement.

God has a way of not allowing us to see anything beyond our next step, anything beyond the next assignment, anything beyond the next instruction (Psalm 119:105). In a sense, He does this to protect us. He has such amazing things planned, that just knowing what is out there could cause us to become proud, lazy, self-centered, or boastful. So, He keeps the ending to himself. He merely asks us to dare to step out of the boat and trust Him even when we can't trace Him.

The Bible says, "And we know that in all things God works for the good of those who love him, who have been called according to his purpose." (Romans 8:28 NIV). This includes those times when people gossip about you. It includes those times when people slander your name or lie about you, and those times when the world feels like it's falling apart. Jesus says, "I'm out here on the water. I'm coming for you. And I dare you to meet Me halfway."

God Is Always on the Winning Side

I'm on the winning side because I choose Christ each and every day. You can be on the winning side, too. When you recognize this, you don't have to worry about tomorrow. You don't have to worry about what comes against you.

Maybe the devil is throwing punches, yet you choose to praise God. Maybe you don't have a dime in the bank, yet you choose joy. Maybe your home is literally falling apart, yet you choose to rest in the house of the Lord. Maybe your job isn't working out, but you know that God is the Source of your strength.

When your life is about believing that Christ is on your side, you live every day believing that He has something good in store for you. You trust Him even when you find that He has led you out onto the lake and nothing is holding you up except for His power and mystery.

Tests of Faith

> *When they climbed back into the boat, the wind stopped. Then the disciples worshiped him. "You really are the Son of God!" they exclaimed.*
>
> ***—Matthew 14:32-33***

I want to point out that there are two very distinct perspectives that we find in the story of Peter walking on water. The first perspective is that of Peter. Once he overcame his shock, he dared to step out and meet Jesus where He was. He dared to show trust and courage. He dared to see beyond the wind and the waves and his earthly circumstances.

Then there is the perspective of the rest of the disciples. They knew Jesus could work miracles—they had just seen one. They had given up everything to follow Him, and yet there they stayed, in the boat. It was as if seeing Him in the distance was not enough to get them to move. They preferred Him right there, in the flesh.

Of course, they still had a lot to learn. They

would soon find out that Jesus would not always be with them, and they would have to rely on His power from afar. But in that moment, they chose the boat, safe from the waves, safe from the depths. They were so safe that they missed out on the incredible experience of walking on water.

Peter took action. The rest of the disciples chose to wait. It wasn't until after Jesus climbed in the boat with Peter and the wind stopped that they exclaimed, "You really are the Son of God!" (Matthew 14:33).

God doesn't want you to be a bystander in life. He wants you to put forth an effort and stop waiting on the preachers, stop waiting on the deacons, stop waiting on the intercessors to bring something into your life. God says it's time for you to open up your sanctified mouth and begin to declare the favor of the Lord for yourself (Luke 4:19).

Life Outside the Boat

The Bible teaches us that God gives us power and authority. He gives us insight (discernment), and according to the writings of Solomon in Proverbs 18:21, we carry a lot of power in what we say. Once we begin to understand our potential and God's power that resides within us, we can start challenging our boundaries.

Paul wrote in Ephesians 3:20 (NIV), "Now to him who is able to do immeasurably more than all we ask or imagine, according to the power that is at work within us." The King James Version uses the phrase "above all that we ask or think." In other words, God has given us the power to do more than we have the ability to imagine, yet many believers live safely in our comfort zones.

Many Christians will never move outside the boat. They'll stay in the boat all their lives, paddling and going nowhere. They'll complain and talk about how much they dislike their circumstances, and yet they wouldn't dare move from where they are.

God is calling for us to live outside the boat. He is calling us to trust Him and to dare to take that step in obedience.

He's walking toward you even now. Won't you meet Him outside the safety of the boat? One of the greatest frustrations is not living up to what God has made available to you. Your willingness to venture outside of the boat will empower your ability to journey far beyond your imagination.

WORKBOOK

Chapter Three Questions

Question: What are the dangers of making decisions based on appearances rather than facts? When is a time that you made a decision based on a momentary perception and later realized that you only had part of the story?

____

____

Question: What are God's motives in His dealings toward you? Why do people sometimes assume that God is working against them? How does a deep relationship with God help to correct your perception of Him?

____

____

____

____

____

____

____

____

____

____

____

____

Question: The disciples, other than Peter, were so safe that they missed out on the incredible experience of walking on water. Do you identify more with Peter, who stepped out in faith, or the disciples who stayed safely in the boat? What do you think made the difference in their responses to seeing Jesus on the water?

Question: What is holding you back from taking a step of faith today? With what action step can you move forward even as you wait for God to reveal the next part of His plan for you?

____

____

____

____

____

____

Action: God sees the end from the beginning. We just see a small glimpse of where we've been and where we are now. Think of someone who has walked with Christ faithfully for many years. Talk to them about the ups and downs of their Christian journey and how they have seen God's faithfulness throughout.

Chapter Three Notes

CONCLUSION

Seek His Face

> We have been snared in the coils of a spurious logic which insists that if we have found Him, we need no more seek Him. ... To have found God and still to pursue Him is the soul's paradox of love, scorned indeed by the too-easily-satisfied religionist, but justified in happy experience by the children of the burning heart.[4]

This life is full of ups and downs. It's full of incredible pain, immense joy, extreme devastation, overwhelming hope, and so much more.

It's easy to let the complexities of life get to us. When this happens, we may begin to focus on chasing pleasure rather than seeking God. We choose sin over following Him, and sometimes that sin is quite enjoyable. It's an escape from whatever haunts us. It's a way out, a way to feel happy, even for just a moment.

When this happens, it can be hard to make the

decision to come back to Christ. The thought of being a “good Christian” isn’t all that appealing, even if we know in our hearts it’s what we need to do.

And so, we put it off. We keep choosing the ways of the world. We live in our sin.

Eventually, though, we get a wakeup call. And when that call happens, we have three choices: we can stay in our sin and reject God completely; we can choose Christ and settle into a safe, comfortable life as an ordinary person; or we can dare to be extraordinary in Christ.

When we choose Christ, it’s easy to go through the motions, to play it safe while we check all the right boxes in hopes that going to church, tithing, and the occasional prayer time will be enough. Then, when a storm hits, when our life is completely turned upside down, we either crumble or we suddenly become spiritual, praying ceaselessly, fasting, seeking God—doing all the things we should have been doing from the start.

God never promised us an easy time here on earth. What He did promise was that He would make a way, that He would declare victory, and that we would be rewarded for our good and faithful service (Matthew 25:23).

But good and faithful service goes far beyond attending church on Sunday.

He Wants More

When You said, "Seek My face," my heart said to You, "Your face, Lord, I will seek."
—*Psalm 27:8* *(NKJV)*

God wants so much more from us. He wants us to follow Him with passion and fervor. He wants us to seek Him in all things, to trust that when He says to get in the boat, the storm won't overcome us, and the waves won't drown us.

God wants this, because when we have that kind of close relationship with Him, that's when we truly can find contentment in the hard times. That's when the storm doesn't look as bad, the army following us doesn't look as fierce, and the water that we are daring to walk upon doesn't frighten us.

In the Bible, we read of incredible things happening to those who dared to go the distance with God. We read of people being healed, armies being defeated, and literal chains being broken. It's easy to look at these stories and assume that they aren't meant for us today: "Surely God doesn't expect us to be able to walk on water in the twenty-first century!"

While He might not be calling you to walk on literal water, He *is* calling you to do something daring, great, and impossible for Him.

You Have Been Called

What is it that God wants you to get out of the boat for? What passion or burden has He placed on your heart? What thought doesn't leave you at night and you keep thinking "what if?"

What if I dare to start a homeless ministry at my church?

What if I dare to give more of my earnings to missionaries and churches?

What if I leave corporate America behind and go after that ministry position that I feel God leading me toward?

What if I invite my neighbors over for dinner?

What if I get rid of cable, Netflix, Hulu, and spend that time serving single mothers?

God calls us to do a range of things for His glory. They may not all seem as faith-testing as walking on water, but only God knows the true impact when we follow through and choose His way over our ways of comfort.

Only God knows the incredible blessing that is in store for us when we dare to get out of the boat.

Dare the Impossible

This is your challenge if you want to experience the incredible power of God working in and through you.

Purge sin from your life, and when you find sin

areas that are difficult to overcome, rely on God more than you've ever relied on Him in the past. He is your ticket to freedom.

Seek Him. Follow Him. Make Him the director of your path. When He says to get into the boat, get into the boat without asking questions or considering what could go wrong.

Trust Him. Understand that He will bring you through whatever earthly trials pop up while you're on His boat. He will rescue and reward you.

Dare to do more. While being in the boat is a great act of love and servitude toward God, daring to get out of the boat, daring to trust Him when He says, "Come, I want you to do this impossible thing," that's when you'll never be the same again.

You'll walk on water. Even if for just a moment. And your eyes will be opened to a side of Christianity that you have never known before.

WORKBOOK

Conclusion Questions

Question: Is your life best described as a life of sin devoid of God, a life of safe and comfortable Christianity, or a life of daring faith and experiencing God's faithfulness?

____

____

____

____

____

____

____

____

____

____

____

Question: What are some of the amazing things God has done through those who were fully committed to Him?

____

____

____

____

____

____

____

____

____

____

____

____

Action: How has God spoken to you as you've read this book? Summarize in two to three sentences what you have learned from this book and how you will put it into action in your life.

____

____

____

____

____

Conclusion Notes

Acknowledgments

As I look back over my life and reflect upon the individuals who have contributed to my development and to the person I've grown to be, I must pause to show appreciation for each contribution.

To the first churches I attended—The Apostolic Church of Jesus in Avon Park, Florida, Malone Memorial Institutional Church of God and Christ, and the Macedonia Missionary Baptist Church—words can't express my gratitude for the deposits you placed into my life and ministry. To my friends and colleagues at Florida A&M University, especially the Gospel Choir, thank you for allowing me to develop my leadership skills. To my boys (musicians) from the Hill: our life experiences have played a significant role in my development. And Rick Watford and Troy Sneed, you pushed me into who I am, not even knowing how God used you to place me in the musical world.

Thank you to the great spiritual leaders from whom I've grown: Pastor Larry C. Miles, Bishop

Joseph W. Walker, Bishop Thomas Brown Sr. (deceased), Bishop Melton L. Scoiners (deceased), Bishop Samuel Green, Mother Mildred Eason (deceased), Mother Willie Mae Pope (deceased), Pastor Sharon Riley, Pastor Barry Stephens, Pastor Alexis Stephens, Bishop Anthony Gilyard, Pastor Cordelia Wallace, Pastor Bryant Townsend, Bishop Shawn Bell, Bishop Herbert Crump, Pastor John P. Kee, Bishop Derrick W. Hutchins, Apostle Dannie Williams, Apostle Andre Alan Williams, Pastor Leroy Rose III, Pastor Willie C Barnes, and last but certainly not least, my mentors and friends, Archbishop Allen T.D. Wiggins and Lady Deborah.

To the greatest church created, The Experience Christian Center family: all of you have made a tremendous impact on my life, and I love and honor each of you. To my executive pastor, Khayree Pender: you've been a friend to me, not just an assistant. To my amazing team of elders, ministers, deacons, mothers, and executive team members: you are so appreciated. We are genuinely "bigger than a Sunday."

To my wonderful parents, Eugene (deceased) and Deitrice Glenn, thank you for the prayers and confidence you spoke over me growing up. To my grandparents, Moses (Billy) and Virginia McRae, thank you for caring and playing such major roles in my life. Eugene (deceased) and Elizabeth Glenn (deceased), thank you for making sure that

I knew my family while my dad and mom were working it out. Darius and Elise'—love you two.

To my children—Brailon, Derrick II, and Kayla—thank you for sacrificing so much to support me.

And to my lovely wife, Taja Chanel: You've made the greatest sacrifice for my success. You believed in me when it was just a vision. I'm forever grateful for you and your willingness to trust the leading of God in me. You've made ministry easier while wearing so many hats. I recognize that none of this would be possible without you. I love you and I appreciate every one of your sacrifices.

About thc Author

Pastor Derrick L. McRae, senior pastor of The Experience Christian Center in Orlando, Florida, hails from the humble origins of Avon Park, Florida. He accepted his call to ministry in 1997 and became licensed under the Church of God in Christ in 1998. He served as youth pastor at Malone Memorial Church of God in Christ for five years and at Macedonia Missionary Baptist for six years. In 2009, at the age of 35, Pastor McRae established and began his pastorate of The Experience Christian Center with twenty-two members.

Currently, the ministry has grown to over 1,600 members and continues to grow at a phenomenal rate. Through positive mentoring, consistent coaching, and on-going support, The Experience Christian Center proudly serves 15,000 people each year through its outreach efforts. It has expanded beyond its original location to three physical locations and seven weekly services. Through social media, Pastor McRae and The Experience Christian Center reach more than 10,500 social media followers each week and continue to grow daily. In nine short years, the Center has expanded to three campuses—Orlando, East Orlando, and the University of Central Florida.

Pastor McRae currently serves as the chaplain at Saints Academy School and as a mentor at Lockhart Middle School. In addition to pastoring and teaching, he serves as the vice president of the African American Council of Christian Clergy. He also serves on the following boards: African American Chamber of Commerce of Central Florida, Orange County Parks and Recreation, and My Brother's Keeper Orlando. Pastor McRae has continued to provide life-changing services to adults and children in need—many of whom may otherwise have been forgotten in today's society.

Pastor McRae's inspiring messages and infectious personality make him a highly sought-after preacher, teacher and motivational speaker. Throughout his life and ministry, Pastor McRae has demonstrated a caliber of leadership and insight beyond his years. Recognized as a teacher, preacher, lecturer, motivational speaker, church growth coach, mentor, talk show host, drummer, radio personality, choir director, and business owner, Pastor Derrick McRae is an anointed man of God whose voice is calling for national and global leadership that enhances the quality of life for all people.

Pastor McRae is the loving husband of Taja C. McRae. They have two sons, Brailon and Derrick II, and one daughter, Kayla.

About Sermon To Book

SermonToBook.com began with a simple belief: that sermons should be touching lives, *not* collecting dust. That's why we turn sermons into high-quality books that are accessible to people all over the globe.

Turning your sermon series into a book exposes more people to God's Word, better equips you for counseling, accelerates future sermon prep, adds credibility to your ministry, and even helps make ends meet during tight times.

John 21:25 tells us that the world itself couldn't contain the books that would be written about the work of Jesus Christ. Our mission is to try anyway. Because in heaven, there will no longer be a need for sermons or books. Our time is now.

If God so leads you, we'd love to work with you on your sermon or sermon series.

Visit www.sermontobook.com to learn more.

REFERENCES

Notes

[1] "Appearance." In *Random House Unabridged Dictionary* (Random House, 2018), quoted in Dictionary.com. http://www.dictionary.com/browse/appearance?s=t.

[2] "Strong's H8615 – tiqvah." In *Strong's Hebrew Lexicon (KJV)*, quoted in Blue Letter Bible. https://www.blueletterbible.org/lang/lexicon/lexicon.cfm?Strongs=H8615&t=KJV.

[3] "Strong's H319 – 'achariyth." In *Strong's Hebrew Lexicon (KJV)*, quoted in Blue Letter Bible. https://www.blueletterbible.org/lang/lexicon/lexicon.cfm?Strongs=H319&t=KJV.

[4] Tozer, A. W. *The Pursuit of God.* Christian Publications, 1982, p. 15–17.

Made in the USA
Coppell, TX
15 December 2020

43868758R00056